Enduring Ties
Healing Through the Honesty of Love

Luz Rivera

Copyright © 2025, Luz Rivera

Copyrights Registration # TX 9 - 535 - 031

ALL RIGHTS RESERVED

No part of this book may be reproduced or transmitted in any form by any means, electronic or mechanical, including photocopying and recording, or by any information storage and retrieval system, except as may be expressly permitted in writing from the author.

ISBN:

Published by: Columbus Book Publishers

www.columbusbookpublishers.com/

Disclaimer:

This book is intended for personal reflection and emotional guidance only. It is not a substitute for professional advice, diagnosis, or therapy. The author shares personal perspectives and insights based on life experience. Readers should seek professional help if they are experiencing emotional distress or mental health concerns.

Dedication

To the ones who dared to love, lost themselves, and want to find their way back.

Table of Contents

Introduction	1
Chapter 1: *The Ones Who Leave Without Warning*	2
Chapter 2: *Loving Someone Who Never Really Saw You*	3
Chapter 3: *Being Blamed for Needing Space*	4
Chapter 4: *Feeling Like You're the Problem*	5
Chapter 5: *Losing Yourself Slowly*	6
Chapter 6: *When He Says You Treat Him Like Sh*t*	7
Chapter 7: *How Silence Is Misunderstood*	8
Chapter 8: *The Emotional Damage of Always Explaining Yourself*	9
Chapter 9: *Starting to See Things Clearly*	10
Chapter 10: *You Were Not Too Much – They Were Too Little*	11
Chapter 11: *Letting Go of the Fantasy*	12
Chapter 12: *The Day You Stopped Chasing Love*	13
Chapter 13: *Breaking the Cycle of Almosts*	14
Chapter 14: *Unlearning What Hurt Taught You*	15
Chapter 15: *Healing is Not Linear*	16
Chapter 16: *Loving Yourself Out Loud*	17
Chapter 17: *Setting Boundaries Without Apologizing*	18
Chapter 18: *You Can Miss Them and Still Move On*	19
Chapter 19: *You Deserve Peace, Not Proof*	20
Chapter 20: *Becoming the Love You Were Looking For*	21
Chapter 21: *Final Letter to the Reader*	22
Chapter 22: *Reflection Pages / Closing Message*	23
Closing Words from the Author	24
About the Author	25

Introduction

Maybe it wasn't love. Maybe it was a lesson.

I wrote this book from a place of pain and clarity. Life, love, and everything in between have their own way of breaking us down and building us back up.

This book is for those who've been misunderstood, mistreated, and left wondering if love was ever real. This is my truth – and if you're holding this book, I hope it becomes a mirror for yours.

Chapter 1

The Ones Who Leave Without Warning

They don't say goodbye. They don't explain. They just vanish.

And you're left trying to piece together what you did wrong. You replay conversations, reread texts, wondering if your love was too much or not enough. The silence they leave behind is louder than anything they ever said.

But the truth is - someone who can leave you like that never truly valued your presence to begin with. You deserved closure. You deserved honesty. You deserved someone who stayed.

Healing starts when you realize their exit wasn't about your worth. It was about their inability to face it.

So don't chase after ghosts.

You are not the reason they disappeared - you are the reason someone better will stay.

Reflection

Have you ever felt abandoned without explanation?
What did that silence teach you about yourself?

Chapter 2

Loving Someone Who Never Really Saw You

Loving someone who never really saw you is one of the loneliest places to be.

They were there in presence but not in spirit. You shared your thoughts, your dreams, your fears, but their eyes never lit up when they looked at you. You were emotionally naked in front of them, and they couldn't even see the courage that took.

It's painful - loving someone who only loved the idea of you.

You're not hard to love. You were just giving your love to someone who was emotionally blind.

Reflection

What does being seen mean to you?

Chapter 3

Being Blamed for Needing Space

When you take space to breathe or protect your peace and someone turns it into blame, that's manipulation.

You're not wrong for needing a moment. You're not selfish for stepping back. If your silence makes someone more uncomfortable than their behavior did, they were never listening to you - only controlling you.

Don't apologize for honoring your own voice. That's how you begin healing - by hearing yourself clearly.

Reflection

Do you allow yourself space without guilt?

Chapter 4

Feeling Like You're the Problem

When you love someone who's not healing, they'll start to project their pain onto you.

You begin to carry weight that doesn't belong to you. You try harder, love louder, and shrink yourself, thinking maybe it'll make things easier.

But love should not feel like punishment.

Feeling like you're the problem when all you wanted was to be loved - that's emotional trauma. And healing is walking away from that guilt.

Reflection

Where did that false belief begin for you?

Chapter 5

Losing Yourself Slowly

It happens slowly. You stop doing the things you loved. You question your worth. You silence your needs. And you keep making excuses for why they don't show up for you.

That's how it starts - the slow erosion of your spirit in the name of love.

But love that costs your peace is not love - it's dependency. And you are worth so much more than that.

Reflection

In what ways have you given yourself away in the name of love?

Chapter 6

When He Says You Treat Him Like Sh*t

You withdraw to protect your peace, and suddenly you're the villain in his story. Silence isn't cruelty - sometimes it's survival.

Suddenly, your love is seen as harm. Your efforts dismissed. Your pain overlooked.

Sometimes they project their guilt onto you so they don't have to face themselves.

But you know your heart... and you know what you gave.

Don't let false accusations rewrite the truth of your love.

Reflection

Have you ever been shamed for protecting your peace? What did it teach you?

Chapter 7

How Silence Is Misunderstood

Silence isn't always punishment. Sometimes it's protection.

You stayed quiet to keep the peace, to avoid the fight, to hold yourself together. But they didn't see that.

They called you cold. Distant. Dismissive.

They never asked what you needed. They just assumed. And that silence they judged was actually your strength.

Reflection

What does silence mean to you – safety, fear, or something else?

Chapter 8

The Emotional Damage of Always Explaining Yourself

Having to explain every emotion, every reaction, every sigh - it's exhausting. Especially when your truth is being dismissed.

You were always trying to be understood while they refused to understand. That's not love - that's survival.

It emotionally wears you down, makes you doubt yourself. You weren't too complicated - they were unwilling to listen.

Reflection

When was the last time you felt truly listened to?
What did that moment feel like?

Chapter 9

Starting to See Things Clearly

It hits you in pieces - the truth. You replay moments and realize how little you were truly seen. And the fog starts to lift.

You weren't crazy. You weren't needy. You were hurting and unheard.

Clarity doesn't come overnight, but once it begins, it can't be stopped.

Reflection

What clarity have you recently gained about a relationship or your worth?

Chapter 10

You Were Not Too Much – They Were Too Little

They said you were too much. But what they meant was - you felt too deeply, you loved too loudly, you expected honesty.

You weren't too much - they were too little.

Let that sink in, and don't ever shrink again for someone with small hands and a smaller heart.

Reflection

What part of yourself have you been hiding to make others comfortable?

Chapter 11

Letting Go of the Fantasy

You were in love with a version of them that only existed in your mind.

The fantasy kept you hoping. The reality kept hurting.

Letting go doesn't mean you stop caring. It means you stop lying to yourself.

Reflection

What fantasy were you holding onto? How did letting it go bring you peace?

Chapter 12

The Day You Stopped Chasing Love

You begged, you waited, you hoped. Until one day, you didn't.

That day was quiet, powerful. The storm inside you finally passed.

You stopped chasing someone who never truly saw your worth.

You didn't lose - you finally walked away from the lie.

Reflection

What did choosing yourself look like for the first time?

Chapter 13

Breaking the Cycle of Almosts

Almost healed. Almost loved. Almost seen.

You deserve more than "almosts."

Break that cycle. Walk into wholeness.

Let "almost" be a word you never settle for again.

Reflection

Where in your life have you settled for "almost?"

What would "absolutely" look like instead?

Chapter 14

Unlearning What Hurt Taught You

You believed love was about sacrificing, proving, enduring. But that belief was built in pain.

Unlearn the things that taught you love meant struggle.

Love is not meant to hurt. Real love does not ask you to bleed to prove it's real.

Reflection

What belief are you ready to release that no longer serves your healing?

Chapter 15

Healing is Not Linear

Some days you'll feel strong. Some days you'll cry again. That's okay.

Healing is not a straight road. It loops, it pauses, it climbs.

Give yourself grace for the days you feel heavy. You're still healing. You're still moving.

Reflection

How do you show yourself compassion when the healing journey feels messy?

Chapter 16

Loving Yourself Out Loud

Say it out loud: "I love me."

Say it again when it's hard. Again when you're lonely. Again when you want to call them back.

Because the loudest love should always come from you.

Reflection

What would it look like to love yourself unapologetically?

Chapter 17

Setting Boundaries Without Apologizing

"No" is a full sentence.

You don't need to explain why you don't want to be treated badly, disrespected, or ignored.

Set the boundary. Walk in peace. Let others adjust or walk away – either is a blessing.

Reflection

Where in your life do you still feel guilt for setting a boundary?

Chapter 18

You Can Miss Them and Still Move On

You can cry for them and still close the door.

You can miss the laughter, the warmth, and even the version of them you once believed in—and still choose silence when they call.

Missing them doesn't mean you're not healing. It means you're human.

Let yourself miss them - just don't go back.

Reflection

What are you still holding onto that you've already outgrown?

Chapter 19

You Deserve Peace, Not Proof

You don't have to prove your worth at all, especially while you're going through pain.

You deserve a love that feels like calm, not chaos.

A love that brings peace without needing proof.

Reflection

What proof have you been trying to earn that was never yours to chase?

Chapter 20

Becoming the Love You Were Looking For

- You are the healing.
- Become the safe space.
- Become the deep love.
- Become the peace.
- Become the loyalty to thyself.
- Be what you need, and let that love find you.

Reflection

How can you start showing up for yourself the way you've shown up for others?

Chapter 21

Final Letter to the Reader

To the reader...

If you made it this far, you're stronger than you realize. This wasn't just a book. This book is your mirror. It is the truth, pain, and healing wrapped in paper. I hope you see yourself. I hope you forgive yourself, and I hope you choose yourself.

Most of all, I hope love - the real kind - finds you when you least expect it, and when you most deserve it.

A reminder that you can survive heartbreak and come home to yourself - stronger, softer, wiser. Thank you for walking through these pages with me.

Chapter 22

Reflection Pages / Closing Message

This is your healing space. Write your heart out. Be honest. Let it go.

Take a moment to reflect:

- What did you learn about your love patterns?
- Where did you feel seen or called out?
- What boundaries will you now honor?
- What truth do you need to accept?

This book isn't just mine. It's yours now too.

With love,
Luz Rivera

Closing Words from the Author

Thank you for reading these pages – for walking through the pain, the clarity, and the healing with me.

If any part of this book felt like your own story, know that you're not alone. You are not broken – you are growing.

May you never again question your worth. May you fall in love with yourself over and over again.

This isn't the end. This is your new beginning.

With love,
– Luz Rivera

About the Author

Born in Puerto Rico and raised in New York, Luz Rivera writes from a place of truth and lived experience. Her journey through cycles of pain and self-discovery led her to a deeper mission: helping others find clarity through love and self-worth.

Luz hopes this book gives readers strength to remember that loving yourself first is the foundation for receiving love from others.

Fun fact:
Relationships can be confusing and complicated, but so is trying to figure out what to wear the next day.

www.ingramcontent.com/pod-product-compliance
Lightning Source LLC
Chambersburg PA
CBHW050733010526
44107CB00010B/835